S0-CBN-049

SAGUARO
voices

WESTERN NATIONAL PARKS ASSOCIATION

Western National Parks Association supports parks across the West, developing products, services, and programs that enrich the visitor experience. WNPA is a nonprofit partner of the National Park Service.

Western National Parks Association
12880 North Vistoso Village Drive
Tucson, Arizona 85755
www.wnpa.org

Edited by Stephanie Hester
Designed by Sandy Bell Design, Springdale, Utah
Printed in China

FIRST EDITION
17   16   15   14   13   1   2   3   4   5

Library of Congress Cataloging-in-Publication Data

Saguaro voices / edited by Stephanie Hester. — First Edition.
    pages cm
  ISBN 978-1-58369-168-7 (hardcover)
  1. Saguaro—Quotations, maxims, etc. 2. National parks and reserves—United States—Quotations, maxims, etc. I. Hester, Stephanie, editor. II. Western National Parks Association.
  QK495.C11S24 2013
  583'.56—dc23
                2013027366

These are remnants of a culture we now call "Hohokam." ... From 200 to 1450 AD farmers lived in villages near Saguaro National Park, venturing into both the Rincon and Tucson Mountains to hunt and gather native foods to supplement their dry-farmed crops of corn, beans, and squash. Their ingenuity and ability to survive and even thrive in the harsh desert amazes us.

NATIONAL PARK SERVICE, 2013

7

Whereas a certain area within the Catalina Division of the Coronado National Forest in the State of Arizona and certain adjacent lands are of outstanding scientific interest because of the exceptional growth thereon of various species of cacti, including the so-called giant cactus ... the public interest will be promoted by reserving as much land as may be necessary for the proper protection thereof as a national monument.

PRESIDENT HERBERT HOOVER,
PROCLAMATION CREATING SAGUARO
NATIONAL MONUMENT, 1933

It did not take me long in the desert to realize
   I was thinking like a person, and on that score
was deeply outnumbered.

BARBARA KINGSOLVER, *HIGH TIDE IN TUCSON*, 1995

And nowhere is water so beautiful as in the desert,

for nowhere else is it so scarce. By definition. Water,

like a human being or a tree or a bird or a song,

gains value by rarity, singularity, isolation.

In a humid climate, water is common.

In the desert each drop is precious.

EDWARD ABBEY, *DESERT SOLITAIRE*, 1968

It is real desert people who lift their faces

upward with the first signs of moisture.

They know how to inhale properly.

Recognizing the aroma of creosote in the distance.

Relieved the cycle is beginning again.

OFELIA ZEPEDA, *WHERE CLOUDS ARE FORMED*, 2008

15

If you don't die of thirst, there are blessings in the desert. You can be pulled into limitlessness, which we all yearn for, or you can do the beauty of minutiae, the scrimshaw of tiny and precise. The sky is your ocean, and the crystal silence will uplift you like great gospel music, or Neil Young.

ANNE LAMOTT, 2004

The desert in bloom is a wonderful sight to behold.

DORIS EVANS, SAGUARO NATIONAL PARK, 2006

Clouds skim high overhead, untouchable,

unknowable.

Most days, rainfall is a mere rumor,

a phenomenon read of in books.

JANICE EMILY BOWERS, *THE MOUNTAINS NEXT DOOR*, 1991

Even desert creatures come from
a time older than the woodland
animals, and they, in answer to the
arduousness, have retained prehistoric
coverings of chitin and lapped scale
and primitive defenses of spine
and stinger, fang and poison, shell
and claw.

WILLIAM LEAST HEAT-MOON, *BLUE HIGHWAYS:
A JOURNEY INTO AMERICA*, 1982

Sky islands [in Saguaro National Park]—verdant mountain ranges rising dramatically from the barren valley floor—are as much as 30 degrees cooler than the surrounding desert. . . . [Hiking to and from the sky islands] you rise and fall through six different ecosystems of cacti and pines rife with mountain lions and bears, and vistas so long you'll swear you can see the curvature of the earth.

DAVID PIDGEON, 2008

…the giant cactus, or saguaro…
It is this strange plant, more than
any other, that gives the key-note
to the landscape, and that most
strongly impresses upon the
mind of the traveler the fact that
this is another world!

WILLIAM TEMPLE HORNADAY, *CAMP-
FIRES ON DESERT AND LAVA,* 1908

27

Most of the birds show no outward signs that they live

in a land of little rain, and the quail who sit thirty feet up

in the saguaro, pecking moisture from its fruit, look,

on the ground, as sleek as their cousins

who drink when they like.

JOSEPH KRUTCH, *THE DESERT YEAR*, 1951

The fruit of the saguaro cactus ripens in late June or early July. O'odham women and children traditionally decamped to a cactus grove for a few weeks to harvest the juicy red fruits. They would knock them from the tops of the tall cacti using a *qwipat*, a long-handled tool fashioned of dried saguaro ribs, and cook them down to a syrup that they could carry home in jars.

TYCHE HENDRICKS, *THE WIND DOESN'T NEED A PASSPORT*, 2010

Even if you don't gather the desert,
let it gather a feeling in you.
Even if you don't swallow it as
medicine, meditate upon it:
the desert can cure.

GARY PAUL NABHAN, *GATHERING THE DESERT*, 1985

33

I found a Gila monster lizard outside the fence. . . .
Beaded in jet black and coral,
the big lizard was breathtaking in his beauty
and a blessing to see.

LESLIE MARMON SILKO, *THE TURQUOISE LEDGE: A MEMOIR*, 2010

We need to weave together the separate threads of
knowledge about the plants and their natural setting
into a close fabric of understanding in which
it will be possible to see the whole pattern
and design of desert life.

FORREST SHREVE, 1936

Now, by any measure

    [the saguaro cactus] is an

  oddball of a plant.

GREGORY MCNAMEE, *A DESERT BESTIARY:*
FOLKLORE, LITERATURE, AND ECOLOGICAL
THOUGHT FROM THE WORLD'S DRY PLACES,
1996

There is nothing so American as our national parks. The scenery and wildlife are native. The fundamental idea behind the parks is native. It is, in brief, that the country belongs to the people, that it is in process of making for the enrichment of the lives of all of us. The parks stand as the outward symbol of this great human principle.

PRESIDENT FRANKLIN D. ROOSEVELT, 1934

Here, harsh weather

    and a harsh land lead

  to few species and

      extraordinary adaptations.

GEORGE OLIN, *HOUSE IN THE SUN: A NATURAL HISTORY OF THE SONORAN DESERT*, 1994

The day fades like other spring days as the evening robs the desert of its color. The distant silhouettes of still-standing saguaros have lost the crisp greenness of morning. They rise darkly against the sky, slightly askew, like Indian totems abandoned by men for centuries.

JOHN ALCOCK, *SONORAN DESERT SPRING,* 1994

PHOTOGRAPHY CREDITS

FRONT COVER; page 35: George H. H. Huey
BACK COVER INSET; pages 42–43: Cameron Rognan
DUST JACKET FLAP DETAILS; pages 10–11; 44–45:
    Jack Dykinga
page 1; 20: Tim Fitzharris/Minden Pictures
pages 2–3: Buddy Mays/Corbis
pages 4–5; 8–9; 24–25: Susan Cole Kelly
pages 6–7: Paul Gill
page 13: Elias Ochoa*
pages 14–15: spirit of america/Shutterstock.com
pages 16–17: J. Norman Reid/Shutterstock.com
page 18: Nigel French/Shutterstock.com
page 19; 32–33: Thomas Wiewandt/
    wildhorizons.com
pages 22–23: Ann and Rob Simpson
pages 26–27; 48: Galyna Andrushko/
    Shutterstock.com
page 28: Steve and Dave Maslowski
page 29: Steve Kaufman/Corbis
page 30: *Arizona Republic*, September 2011
    © Gannett-CN
page 31: Mamta Popat/*Arizona Daily Star*
page 36: Ron Niebrugge/Wild Nature Images
pages 38–39: Kevin Schafer/Minden Pictures
pages 40–41: Lee Daniels
pages 46–47: Richard Hamilton Smith/Corbis

*Elias Ochoa composed this beautiful
photograph at the age of thirteen after hiking
five miles into the Saguaro Wilderness as a
participant of the Udall Foundation's Parks
in Focus program. Parks in Focus connects
youth to nature through photography and
positive outdoor experiences.